GOOD
OLD
HARRY

GOOD
OLD
HARRY

The Wit and Wisdom of
HARRY S TRUMAN

compiled by
GEORGE S CALDWELL

Hawthorn Books, Inc.
Publishers, New York City

First Edition, July, 1966

Photos: *Wide World Photos, Inc.*

Acknowledgment is made to the Columbia University Press for permis-
sion to quote passages from the 1959 lecture series, which was published
under the title *Truman Speaks* © 1959 by Harry S Truman.

The people of the United States love and voted for Harry Truman not because he gave them hell but because he gave them hope.

Lyndon Johnson
Independence, Missouri
July 30, 1965

POLITICAL CAREER

Asked why people in political audiences always call out, "Give 'em hell, Harry," Truman replied:

Well, that started out in the Northwest, in Seattle, Washington. It was in 1948, and we were holding an enthusiastic meeting there when some man with a great big voice cried from the galleries, "Give 'em hell, Harry!" I told him at that time, and I have been repeating it ever since, that I have never deliberately given anybody hell. I just tell the truth on the opposition—and they think it's hell.

Mr. Citizen
by Truman, 1960

If they want to ask me some impudent questions, I'll try to give them some impudent answers.

Lecture series
Columbia University
April 27, 1959

You don't get any double-talking from me. I'm either for something or against it, and you know it. You know what I stand for.

Sparks, Nevada
September 22, 1948

THE SENATE

In late 1934, Harry Truman, the newly elected Senator from Missouri, went to Washington to look over the city where he would reside during the next six years. When he returned to Missouri, he delivered a speech at the Kansas City Elks Club.

My trouble is that I probably won't find a place to live. You see, I have to live on my salary, and a cubbyhole rents for a hundred and fifty dollars a month there. The ones that are fit to live in run from two hundred and fifty to five hundred a month, and, although it's hard to believe, there are some saphead Senators who pay fifteen hundred dollars a month for their apartments.

In a press interview during his first years in Washington, a reporter asked him why he was so reluctant to join in Senate debate. He replied:

I'm not going to demagogue until I have something to demagogue about.

In 1938 he was driving to Kansas City, when the Roosevelt Administration had him hauled back to Washington by the highway police. They needed him to break a tie vote on a major bill. He exploded.

Who do those so-and-sos think they are? I haven't been recognized by the White House, but they think they can use me to vote for Roosevelt! . . . I'm sick and tired of being the White House office boy! This is the third time I've come back here to bail you guys out on a vote. You tell that to the President!

Throughout Truman's political career, critics attacked him for his early association with the Pendergast machine.

When a leader is in the Democratic Party he's a boss, when he's in the Republican Party he's nothing but a leader. But there's no difference.

Lecture series
Columbia University
April 28, 1959

T. J. Pendergast said once of him, "He's the contrariest man on earth." But when Truman was asked why he remained faithful to Pendergast, he replied:

We don't play halfway politics in Missouri. When we start out with a man, if he is any good at all, we always stay with him to the end. Sometimes people quit me but I never quit people when I start to back them up.

From his letters and memoranda of 1949
in Mr. President
by William Hillman

About his days in the Pendergast machine:

I was about as popular as a skunk in the parlor.

VICE-PRESIDENT AND PRESIDENT

On July 18, 1944, on the eve of the Democratic Convention in Chicago, Bob Hannegan, the National Chairman, called on Truman. He told him that the time was approaching for him to withdraw his support from Jimmy Byrnes for the vice-presidency and to declare that he was a candidate. Hannegan now insisted that President Roosevelt wanted Truman as his running mate. Truman's reply was brief.

Tell him to go to hell. I'm for Jimmy Byrnes.

By the end of the week, however, he accepted the nomination for Vice-President and told reporters:

I never ran for a political office I wanted. But I've fought for every one I've ever had. Damn it! I've never had an office I didn't have to fight for, tooth and nail.

On April 11, 1945, when the Senate adjourned for the day, newsmen surrounded Vice-President Truman for an interview. One of the reporters accidentally called him "Mr. President." Truman grinned.

Boys, those are fighting words out in Missouri where I come from. You'd better smile when you say that! You know right here is where I've always wanted to be, and only place I ever wanted to be. The Senate—that's just my speed and my style.

This interview was Truman's last as Vice-President. The following day, April 12, 1945, Franklin D. Roosevelt died.

On April 13, 1945—Truman's first full day as President— he told reporters:

Boys, if you ever pray, pray for me now. I don't know whether you fellows ever had a load of hay fall on you, but when they told me yesterday what had happened, I felt like the moon, the stars, and all the planets had fallen on me.

In 1946, when a Republican Congress was elected, there was a very highly educated Senator, an Oxford graduate, who made the statement that he thought I should appoint a Secretary of State . . . who was in sympathy with Congress. [At that time, the Secretary of State was next in succession after the Vice-President.] Then, he wanted me to resign and said that if I got out the country could run much better than it would otherwise. Well, I said that I thought it would have been a good thing if this able Senator had been educated in a land-grant college in the United States, because then he'd know something about our government.

Lecture series
Columbia University
April 27, 1959

Frustrated by attempts to thwart his proposal to establish a unified Department of Defense, he wrote a letter in 1946 which he never mailed.

Some of the generals and the admirals and the career men in government look upon the occupant of the White House as only a temporary nuisance who soon will be succeeded by another temporary occupant who won't find out what it is all about for a long time and then it will be too late to do anything about it.

That Man from Missouri
by Alfred Steinberg

Well, I had to fire Henry today, and of course I hated to do it. Henry Wallace is the best Secretary of Agriculture this country ever had. . . . If Henry had stayed Secretary of Agriculture in 1940 as he should have, there'd never have been all this controversy, and I would not be here, and wouldn't that be nice? Charlie Ross said I'd rather be right than President, and I told him I'd rather be anything than President.

Letter to his mother and sister Mary
September 20, 1946
in Memoirs of Harry S Truman

In March of 1947, while on a good-will tour of Mexico, President Truman was asked by President Alemán what he thought of the Parícutin volcano.

Frankly, it's nothing compared to the one I'm sitting on in Washington.

In earlier years, I came to Chicago on shopping trips with Mrs. Truman. I enjoyed looking in the windows. No one paid any attention to me then. I suppose a lot of people wish I was looking in the windows again. But they won't get their way because a year from now I'm going to be right back in the same trouble I'm in now.

Speech at a banquet
Palmer House
Chicago
June, 1948

On the twenty-sixth of July, which out in Missouri we call "Turnip Day," I am going to call Congress back and ask them to pass laws to halt rising prices, to meet the housing crisis—which they are saying they are for in their platform.

At the same time, I shall ask them to act upon other vitally needed measures, such as aid to education, which they say they are for; a national health program; civil rights legislation, which they say they are for; an increase in the minimum wage, which I doubt very much they are for; extension of the social security coverage and increased benefits, which they say they are for; funds for projects needed in our program to provide public power and cheap electricity. By indirection this Eightieth Congress has tried to sabotage the power policies the United States has pursued for fourteen years. . . . Now, my friends, if there is any reality behind that Republican platform, we ought to get some action from a short session of the Eightieth Congress. They can do this job in fifteen days, if they want to do it. They will still have time to go and run for office. . . . They are going to drag all the red herrings they can across this campaign, but I am here to say that Senator Barkley and I are not going to let them get away with it.

Acceptance speech
Democratic National Convention
Philadelphia
July 16, 1948

Attacking Dewey for "me-tooism":

It sounds like the same old phonograph record; but this year the record has a crack, and the needle gets stuck in it.

The crack was provided by the Republican Eightieth Congress.

In 1948, every time the candidate says, "I can do it better," the crack says, "We're against it."

Campaign speech
October 24, 1948

Another thing about Mr. Dewey is this. He's for the future. In a speech prepared for delivery at Phoenix, Arizona, he said, "You know your future is still ahead of you." I was greatly impressed by this bold stand of the Republican candidate. It reminds me of a little poem we learned as school children:

> There is nothing here but the present
> Nothing behind but the past,
> Nothing ahead but the future,
> Mi Gosh, how long will it last?

New York City
October 29, 1948

About a speech of Dewey's:

This soft talk and double talk, this combination of crafty silence and resounding misrepresentation, is an insult to the intelligence of the American voter. It proceeds upon the assumption that you can fool all the people—or enough of them—all the time.

Campaign speech
October 24, 1948

Herbert Hoover once ran on the slogan, "Two cars in every garage." Apparently the Republican candidate this year is running on the slogan, "Two families in every garage."

Chicago Stadium
October, 1948

During the 1948 campaign a goat raiser presented Truman with a kid goat wearing the label "Dewey's Goat." Truman's response:

I'll clip it and make a rug out of it, and then I'll let it graze on the White House lawn for the next four years.

San Antonio
September 26, 1948

The Republican doctrine:

If you can't convince them, confuse them.

North Carolina State Fair
Raleigh
October 19, 1948

About Republican candidates:

They dare not answer me. They are afraid to get on the issues. They talk about home, and mother, what a nice country it is, "you can trust us."
You can't trust 'em.

Campaign speech
October 7, 1948

You remember the Hoover cart—the remains of the old Tin Lizzie being pulled by a mule because you couldn't afford to buy a new car or gas for the old one. First you had the Hoovercrats and then you had the Hoover carts. One always follows the other.

By the way, I asked the Department of Agriculture at Washington to look up the pedigree of this Hoover cart. They said it is the only automobile in the world that eats oats. They don't recommend it. Neither do I.

Campaign speech
Raleigh
October 19, 1948

About Republican campaign promises:

The leopard has not changed his spots—he has merely hired some public relations experts. And they have taught him to wear sheep's clothing and to purr sweet nothings about unity in a soothing voice. But it's the same old leopard.

Buffalo
October 8, 1948

I will tell you how you can achieve unity in a headlong dash toward another depression . . . just shut your eyes and vote Republican.

Campaign speech
Charleston, West Virginia
October 1, 1948

Polls are like sleeping pills designed to lull the voters into sleeping on election day. You might call them sleeping polls.

The same doctor I told you about the other night in Pittsburgh—the Republican candidate—keeps handing out these sleeping polls, and some people have been taking them. . . . But most of the people are not being fooled. They know that sleeping polls are bad for the system. They affect the mind. An overdose could be fatal.

Cleveland
October 26, 1948

And now the Republicans tell us that they stand for unity. In the old days, Al Smith would have said, "That's baloney." Today I think he'd say, "That's a lot of hooey." And if that rhymes with anything it's not my fault.

Boston
October 27, 1948

While on his campaign whistle-stop tour, one woman yelled out to him, "Mr. Truman, you sound as if you have a cold." He called back:

That's because I ride around in the wind with my mouth open.

In 1946 two thirds of you stayed home and didn't vote. We got that awful Eightieth Congress as a result. And you got just what you deserved because you didn't exercise your rights!

Newark
October 7, 1948

They [the Republicans] tell you, "We know the Democrats got you out of the last depression that we got you into, but they didn't do it so well and we can do it better."

The Republicans tell you, "We are all for labor's right to collective bargaining which the Democrats gave you, but we know better how it ought to work. . . ."

They don't talk much at election time about how they fought against these great progressive measures tooth and nail. They just say, "Turn all these Democratic programs over to us and we will take care of everything. Just leave everything up to the Republican Party and you won't have anything to worry about."

Do you know what that sounds like to me? It sounds like a "company union." It sounds like one of these generous employers who say to the men and women who work for them, "You don't need to form a union. I'll do it for you—and the union I give you will be better than yours because we won't be fighting with each other."

Campaign speech
Philadelphia
October 6, 1948

You people know a great deal about horse races in Lexington, and you know it doesn't matter which horse is ahead or behind at any given moment, it's the horse that comes out ahead at the finish that counts.

Lexington, Kentucky
October 1, 1948

Now—listen to me! On November the second, get up early and go to the polls and be sure you are right by voting the straight Democratic ticket—and I won't be troubled with the housing shortage.

El Paso
September 25, 1948

At the end of his 1948 presidential campaign, Truman returned to Independence. The plane carrying reporters landed at the airport after he had already started off by car for home. They raced after him in press cars, preceded by a police escort, but when they reached his home, he was not there. He finally arrived several minutes later, and a reporter asked him why he was late.

Oh, we were stopped by a police car and had to pull over. Seems there were some very important people going through town.

Independence, Missouri
November 1, 1948

After his 1948 victory:

I've been in many and many election campaigns as you people here in Missouri know. After the election's over I bear no malice or feel badly toward anyone because the fellow who lost feels badly enough without eating crow.

Jefferson City, Missouri
November 4, 1948

On March 6, 1949, Truman left for a vacation in Key West. The press plane was supposed to arrive ahead of the President's, but it was delayed. Truman met the photographers and newsmen at the ramp, welcomed them to Key West, and "interviewed" them.

Truman: Well, where have you been? Where have you been? Come on down. Where's the president of the White House Correspondents Association? I want to ask him a few questions.

A reporter: We have been running as fast as we could.

Truman: You couldn't catch up!

Admiral Leahy: I don't see how they could get that many people in a plane.

Truman: I don't either.

Voices: Here's the president now.

Truman: Where's the band?

("Hail to the Chief" hummed by the crowd)

What about Molotov, Mr. President?

President of Association: Yes. Yes, indeed.

Truman: All right.

President of Association: I agree.

Truman: And no, too?

President of Association: And no, too. On the other hand, perhaps I shouldn't comment on the matter. It is rather difficult to assay at the moment. We have the matter under considerable study.

Truman: What happened to the plane?

President of Association: A minor accident in the air— threw a propeller.

Truman: I am making this interview for Hearst, so you had better be careful.

After an attempt was made on his life while he lived at Blair House, he was asked what he would have done if one of the gunmen had confronted him with weapon in hand. Mr. Truman replied:

Heck, I would have taken the gun away from him, shoved it up his gullet and pulled the trigger.

Washington, D.C.
November 1, 1950

The assassination attempt was made by Puerto Rican nationals who desired the independence of their territorial island. After the attempt, Mr. Truman reiterated a statement he had made in San Juan in 1948 which said:

The Puerto Rican people should have the right to determine for themselves Puerto Rico's political relationship to the continental United States.

Editors are peculiar animals—they throw mud and bricks at you the whole year round—then they make one favorable statement which happens to agree with facts and they think they should be hugged and kissed for it.

From his letters and memoranda of 1951
in Mr. President
by William Hillman

To an audience of newspapermen:

I'm amazed sometimes when I find that some of you disagree with me. When I consider how you disagree among yourselves, I'm somewhat comforted. I'll begin to think that maybe I'm all right anyway.

American Society of Newspaper Editors
Washington, D.C.
April 17, 1948

Whenever the press quits abusing me, I know I'm in the wrong pew.

Washington, D.C.
February 23, 1958

I also hope the next time . . . you will speak to him in the same restrained manner that a sergeant talks to a mule.

From his letters and memoranda of 1950
in Mr. President
by William Hillman

I had no trouble sleeping. . . . I read myself to sleep every night in the White House, reading biography or the troubles of some President in the past.

About presidential responsibility:

It's his privilege to appoint generals—and sometimes to fire them when it's necessary. It's not a pleasant procedure at all. If you'll read through the history of the country, you'll find that James K. Polk had to do that; Abe Lincoln had to do it four times, and one of the fellows—after Lincoln fired him—ran against him for President. It didn't happen in my case.

> *Lecture series*
> *Columbia University*
> *April 27, 1959*

I am sometimes accused of claiming credit for every good thing that happened in the United States while I have been President, and, by the same token, accused of never admitting a mistake.

As for the mistakes, I know that I make them like everybody else does, and I do admit them from time to time. However, it has not seemed necessary for me to spend a great deal of time calling attention to my mistakes because there have always been plenty of people who were willing to do that for me.

> *Philadelphia*
> *September 16, 1952*

During the month of January, 1953, when Truman was
preparing to leave the White House, he told reporters:

If I had known there would be so much work leaving this
place, I'd have run again.

During the last days of his administration, he wrote this note
to his daughter Margaret:

Your dad will never be reckoned among the great. But
you can be sure he did his level best and gave all he had to
his country. There is an epitaph in Boothill Cemetery in
Tombstone, Arizona, which reads, "Here lies Jack Wil-
liams; he done his damndest." What more can a person do?

ELDER STATESMAN

As he turned over the White House to Eisenhower, Tru-
man's official political career had ended, but he continued
to be a strong spokesman for the Democratic Party. This
last phase of his career began in the fall of 1952 as he
campaigned on behalf of Adlai Stevenson.

Ike has a brass halo.
Campaign speech for Adlai Stevenson
October, 1952

The Republicans will be happy to see fair prices, if prices
happen to be fair. If they don't happen to be fair, well,
prosperity is just around the corner.
Grand Forks, North Dakota
September 29, 1952

At a Columbus Day dinner:

If these Republican orators had been living in Columbus' time, I'm sure they would have been among those who believed the world was flat.

In fact, I'm not altogether certain what their views may be on that subject now.

I'm not going to tell you that Columbus would be a Democrat if he were alive this day, although I can't see why he wouldn't be.

Waldorf Astoria
New York City
October 11, 1952

I am exceedingly happy . . . that this is a nonpartisan organization. I am on a partisan trip and I fear I am going to make you a partisan speech, so if you want to throw me out, now is the time to do it.

Waldorf Astoria
New York City
October 11, 1952

He [the Republican candidate] just walks the farm plank —right off the end of it and into deep water.

Grand Forks, North Dakota
September 29, 1952

Now I see a kid back there who has been paid to carry that "I like Ike" sign. Well, I like Ike—I like Ike so well that I would send him back to the Army, if I had the chance. And that's what I'm trying to do.

Wenatchee, Washington
October 3, 1952

With such a record, how in heaven's name can the Republican Party claim credit for the farm program today?

It reminds me of the flea that was on the back of a donkey crossing a bridge. When they got across, the flea said to the donkey, "Boy, we sure did shake that bridge, didn't we?"

Grand Forks, North Dakota
September 29, 1952

"The Government will build the power dams," he [Eisenhower] said, "the Government will do this and that, the Government does everything but come in and wash the dishes for the housewife."

I'm not sure what the accusation is, whether it is that we built the dams or that we didn't wash the dishes.

Hungry Horse Dam, Montana
October 2, 1952

When Eisenhower was about to take over the Presidency, Truman was said to have remarked:

He'll sit here and he'll say, "Do this! Do that!" and nothing will happen. Poor Ike—it won't be a bit like the Army.

About the economic policy of the Eisenhower Administration:

Creeping McKinleyism!

Amalgamated Clothing Workers Convention
Atlantic City
May 13, 1954

After personally leading the campaign against President Eisenhower, Truman came to the Republican President's defense in a struggle he was having with the leadership in Congress.

The President is responsible for the administration of his office. And that means for the administration of the entire executive branch. It is not the business of Congress to run the agencies of government for the President.

Unless this principle is observed, it is impossible to have orderly government. The legislative power will ooze into the executive offices. It will influence and corrupt the decisions of the executive branch. It will affect promotions and transfers. It will warp and twist policies. . . .

To this kind of encroachment it is the duty of the President to say firmly and flatly, "No, you can't do it." The investigative power of Congress is not limitless. . . .

Our government cannot function properly unless the President is master in his own house and unless the executive departments and agencies of the government, including the armed forces, are responsible only to the President.

New York City
May 8, 1954

About military men as Presidents:

They're honorable men. They want to do the right thing, but they've been educated in a manner that's like a horse with blinders on—he sees only one direction right down the road.

Interview with Edward R. Murrow on the
CBS television program See It Now
February 2, 1958

About the Constitutional amendment forbidding any President to serve more than two terms, he said:

They couldn't include me in it because I was the President, and I can be elected as often as I want to be. I'm going to run again when I'm ninety. I've announced that a time or two, and you know, some damn fool looked the situation over and said, "When you're ninety, it's an off year," so I can't even run then. I didn't know I was going to stir up all that trouble. . . .

The people who passed that amendment made a lame duck out of the very man that they might have elected another time, if the voters still hero-worshipped him as they did in the beginning. I don't know whether that's worn off or not—I hope it has.

Lecture series
Columbia University
April 28, 1959

I want all of you to realize how big a job, how hard a job it [the presidency] is—not for my sake, because I am stepping out of it—but for the sake of my successor. He needs the understanding and the help of every citizen. It is not enough for you to come out once every four years and vote for a candidate and then go back home and say, "Well, I've done my part, now let the new President do the worrying." He can't do the job alone.

Farewell address
Washington, D.C.
January 15, 1953

He [Ike] came to see me one time. I said, "Are you going to run for President?" He said, "No, I wouldn't do that." . . . And I said, "Well, if you were running for President, I wouldn't stand in your way." I didn't say I was for him, because I knew he didn't know what he was, Democrat or Republican; and he doesn't yet.

Lecture series
Columbia University
April 28, 1959

Hearing that the Republicans might hold their 1956 convention in San Francisco's Cow Palace, he said:

Don't worry. They'll soon convert the Cow Palace into a hog-run.

About former Presidents:

You know the United States Government turns its Chief Executive out to grass. They're just allowed to starve. . . . If I hadn't inherited some property that finally paid things through, I'd be on relief now.

Interview with Edward R. Murrow on the
CBS television program See It Now
February 2, 1958

Student: Some people suggest that you are getting mellowed and less militant. Is that so?

Truman: Not in the slightest degree. They are trying to make an elder statesman of me, but they will never succeed.

Mr. Citizen
by Truman, 1960

There is no conversation so sweet as that of former political enemies. The way I look at it, I have been blessed in both enemies and friends.

Mr. Citizen
by Truman, 1960

Some of the Presidents were great and some of them weren't. I can say that, because I wasn't one of the great Presidents, but I had a good time trying to be one, I can tell you that.

Lecture series
Columbia University
April 27, 1959

FAMILY

Once a reporter remarked to Harry Truman that his father, John Anderson Truman, had led a frustrating life and had been a failure. Truman snapped angrily:

My father was not a failure. After all, he was the father of a President of the United States.

I tried to get into military service before I was twenty-one, but could not do so because my mother and father were reconstructed southerners, and they were afraid I would have to wear a blue uniform.

Mr. Citizen
by Truman, 1960

About his mother:

One of the funniest things she said when I brought her to Washington in the plane and got her off at the airport and all the photographers and newsmen crowded around her was, "Oh, fiddlesticks, why didn't you tell me about this, and I would have stayed home."

As he spoke at a dedication ceremony in his home town unveiling a replica of the Liberty Bell, Truman glanced down the street at his childhood church.

You know, I went to Sunday school right across there, the first time in my life, a long long time ago. And in that Sunday school class I met a little blue-eyed, golden-haired girl—my first sweetheart. Her eyes are still blue, but her hair is no longer golden; it's silver, like mine. And she is still my sweetheart.

Independence, Missouri
November 6, 1950

Truman spoke often of his first years with his blue-eyed sweetheart, Bess Wallace.

From the fifth grade in school, which was taught by her Aunt Nannie, until I graduated from high school we were in the same classes. If I succeeded in carrying her books to school or back home for her I had a big day.

I do not know whether Presidents ought to have any descendants, because their descendants inherit the difficult burden of having people expect them to live up to their ancestors.

Mr. Citizen
by Truman, 1960

During the 1944 campaign for the vice-presidency, when Clare Boothe Luce made some critical remarks about Bess, Truman told a reporter:

The way she talked about my wife—well, if she were a man, I would have done something about it.

In 1945 Henry Luce went to the White House to ask why his wife was barred. As reported by Harry Vaughan, Truman replied:

Mr. Luce, you've asked a fair question and I'll give you a fair answer. I've been in politics thirty-five years and everything that could be said about a human being has been said about me. But my wife has never been in politics. She has always conducted herself in a circumspect manner and no one has a right to make derogatory remarks about her. Now your wife has said many unkind and untrue things about Mrs. Truman. And as long as I am in residence here, she'll not be a guest in the White House.

Truman would explode when the press attacked his close associates. Once, after a number of columnists suggested people whom he should fire, he replied:

Everyone is telling me who I should have on my staff and in my Cabinet. No s.o.b. is going to dictate to me who I'm going to have!

Reserve Officers Association
Washington, D.C.
February 23, 1949

Bess was furious with him for using such language in public, but a Washington rector came to his defense, saying that under similar provocation, he might have said the same thing. Truman was only momentarily pleased.

I just wish that rector would go talk to my wife!

Bess and Margaret went to Missouri at 7:30 EDT, 6:30 God's time. I sure hated to see them go. Came back and read the papers, some history and then wrote this. It is hot and humid and lonely. . . .

> *Entry in his diary*
> *From Mr. President*
> *by William Hillman*

I received a card the other day from Steve Early which said, "Don't Worry Me—I am an 8 Ulcer Man on 4 Ulcer Pay."

> *From his letters and memoranda of 1949*
> *in Mr. President*
> *by William Hillman*

In December of 1950 Margaret Truman gave a concert at Constitution Hall in Washington. A review by music critic Paul Hume in the Washington Post the next morning infuriated Truman—especially his remarks, "She is flat a good deal of the time," "She cannot sing with anything approaching professional finish," and "She communicates almost nothing of the music she presents." Truman wrote the following note to Hume:

I have just read your lousy review buried in the back pages. You sound like a frustrated man that never made a success, an eight-ulcer man on a four-ulcer job, and all four ulcers working.

I never met you, but if I do you'll need a new nose and plenty of beefsteak and perhaps a supporter below. Westbrook Pegler, a guttersnipe, is a gentleman compared to you. You can take that as more of an insult than a reflection on your ancestry.

A frustrated critic on the Washington Post wrote a lousy review. The only thing, General Marshall said, he didn't criticize was the varnish on the piano. He put my baby as low as he could and he made the young accompanist look like a dub.

It upset me and I wrote him what I thought of him. I told him he was lower than Mr. X, and that was intended to be an insult worse than a reflection on his ancestry. I would never reflect on a man's mother because mothers are not to be attacked, although mine was.

Well, I've had a grand time this day. I'm accused of putting my baby who is the apple of my eye in a bad position. I don't think that is so. She doesn't either—thank the Almighty.

Truman's diary, 1950

About the only time I ever acted when I was really out of sorts was when I told a music critic where to get off when he said some mean things about my daughter. If I had thought about it, I probably wouldn't have done it.

Interview with Edward R. Murrow on the
CBS television program See It Now
February 2, 1958

Margaret Truman tells this story about her father. He heard one of her concerts sitting in a box with Helen Traubel, the Metropolitan Opera star. As the program was about to begin, the President leaned over to Miss Traubel.

Don't pay any attention to me when I start to tear up the program. It's awful not to be able to help Margaret up there all alone on the platform.

PUBLIC SERVICE

I am not in favor of erecting memorials to people who are living. I think it bad business because a person may do something before he dies that will make the people want to tear the memorial down.

From his letters and memoranda of 1948
in Mr. President
by William Hillman

And I congratulate you on the ribbons I see here before me. I wish I could sport some of them. I pinned a medal on General MacArthur the other day, and told him I wished I had a medal like that, and he said that it was my duty to give the medals not receive them. That is always the way. About all I receive is the bricks. It's a good thing I have got a pretty hard head or it would have been broken a long time ago.

National Guard
Washington, D.C.
October 26, 1950

Mr. Truman went to a junior livestock show and received a huge blue ribbon as "grand champion." He remarked:

I don't know whether I'm the prize pig or what.
Spokane, Washington
May 11, 1950

Do your duty, and history will do you justice.
Dedication address for monument
to Presidents Jackson, Polk and Andrew Johnson
Raleigh
October 19, 1948

There are those who suggest that all federal employees must bear the burden of always seeming right in addition to being right. I go along with this exacting standard. But I will not allow any man to be punished for not seeming to be right if in fact he is not wrong.

Mr. President
by William Hillman

Upon receiving the Freedom House award, after a number of highly laudatory speeches:

You don't know how overcome I am. You don't know how difficult it is to be present at your own funeral and still be able to walk around.
New York City
April, 1965

If you want an efficient government, why then go someplace where they have a dictatorship and you'll get it.

Lecture series
Columbia University
April 28, 1959

Efficiency alone is not enough in government. . . .

Hitler learned that efficiency without justice is a vain thing.

Democracy does not work that way. Democracy is a matter of faith—a faith in the soul of man—a faith in human rights. . . .

Faith is much more than efficiency. Faith gives value to all things. Without faith, the people perish.

St. Paul
October 13, 1948

Men often mistake notoriety for fame, and would rather be remarked for their vices and follies than not be noticed at all!

From his letters and memoranda of 1950
in Mr. President
by William Hillman

As always, I am just trying to do the job I am supposed to do, and a lot of times, in public service, that is an unusual procedure, so it causes comment.

From his letters and memoranda of 1947
in Mr. President
by William Hillman

When Truman's old friend Roger Sermon, Mayor of Independence, introduced him once by saying simply, "Ladies and gentlemen, the President of the United States," Truman responded:

That was the shortest speech I ever heard you make in all my life. I appreciate that and I know you meant every word of it.

Independence, Missouri
December 26, 1949

About state dinners:

Every time one of those great dinners comes up, you can only seat ninety-nine people in the State Dining Room in the White House, and you know what a time it is to get those ninety-nine places filled . . . without making some of the great old social leaders feel pretty bad because they're not on the list. But sometimes it does them good to be left off; they behave a little better after that.

Lecture series
Columbia University
April 27, 1959

No government is perfect. One of the chief virtues of a democracy, however, is that its defects are always visible and under democratic processes can be pointed out and corrected.

Address to Congress
March 12, 1947

By their votes ye shall know them.

Los Angeles
September 23, 1948

Official records designate Truman as the thirty-third President. He disagrees.

I am the thirty-second man to be President. If you count the administrations of Grover Cleveland twice because another President held office between Cleveland's first and second terms, you might try to justify the designation of me as thirty-third President. But then why don't you number all the second terms of other Presidents and the third and fourth terms of President Roosevelt, and where will you be? I am the thirty-second President.

Mr. President
by William Hillman

When Truman called the President of the United States the lobbyist for all 160 million people, he was asked if the President's real obligations weren't to those who voted for him—to those of his own party.

No! His obligations are to the country, and when he meets those obligations, there'll be more out of that 160 million that will vote for him next time.

Lecture series
Columbia University
April 27, 1959

Whenever you put a man on the Supreme Court, he ceases to be your friend, you can be sure of that.

Lecture series
Columbia University
April 28, 1959

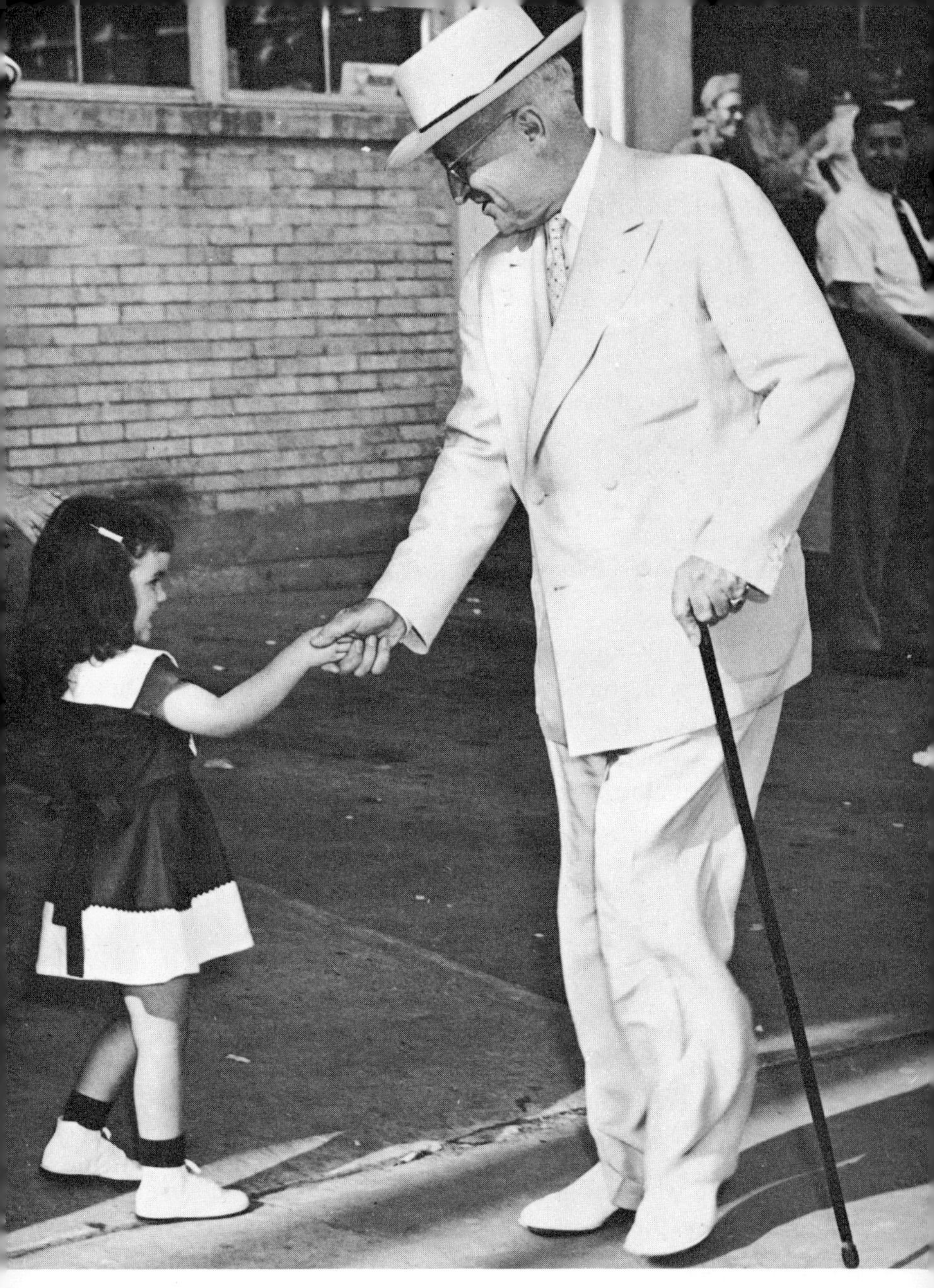

About how a Senator could become President:

Be very shy and aloof, say you want to go home and write your memoirs. Say you would not touch the crown with a ten-foot pole—refuse it at least thrice—but say nothing about just taking it in hand and wearing it at the proper time. This method may bring home the bacon.

Gridiron Club
Washington, D.C.
May 11, 1947

Asked whether he thought a woman would ever be President:

Well, it's not beyond the bounds of possibility. We are almost a matriarchy now. The women control the finances of the country. They could do it. There isn't any doubt but what a woman would make a good President. They make good Senators, good members of the House of Representatives and have held other important offices in the Government of the United States.

NBC panel discussion
Waldorf Astoria
January 10, 1954

During one of Truman's Cabinet meetings, Vice-President Barkley observed that where poverty goes in the front door, love goes out the transom. Barkley recalled later that Truman added:

And where politics goes in the front door, statesmanship flies out the transon.

That Man from Missouri
by Alfred Steinberg

LABOR RELATIONS

John L. Lewis: When you call me a demagogue, I will say you are less than a proper representative of the common people of this country when you do that.

Truman (chairman of the investigating committee): Now, Mr. Lewis, we don't stand for any sassy remarks to the members of this committee, and your rights will be protected here just the same as those of everybody else. I don't like that remark to a member of this committee.

Mr. Lewis: Senator, did you object when the Senator [Joseph H. Ball] called me a demagogue?

Truman: Yes, it works both ways. I don't think the Senator should have called you a demagogue.

Mr. Lewis: Who cast the first stone?

Truman: I'm stopping it right now.

Congressional hearings
March 26, 1943

When a machine replaces ten men, the machine must reabsorb the men by providing each with, say, two hours a day of work, for which they should receive the living wage of former years. . . .

In the past the profits of the machine have been going to the machine owner. It seems to me that now the profits must be divided more equally with labor.

Speech to Roosevelt Progressive Democrats
Kansas City, Missouri
February 10, 1934

About tight money:

It reflects a reversion to the old idea that the tree can be fertilized at the top instead of at the bottom—the old trickle-down theory.

Amalgamated Clothing Workers Convention
Atlantic City
May 13, 1954

Your old friend Congressman Hartley of the Taft-Hartley team . . . has written a book. . . . The title of this book is *Our New National Labor Policy, the Taft-Hartley Act and the Next Steps.*

Get that: "The Next Steps" . . . They're going even further!

Akron
October 11, 1948

The Republicans favor a minimum wage—the smaller the minimum the better.

Akron
October 11, 1948

In 1937 Truman was chairman of a Senate committee for investigating the financial setup of the railroads. During this period he made his first important speeches in the Senate. He called the railroad financiers "wrecking crews," and Wall Street lawyers the "highest of high hats" who pulled "tricks that would make an ambulance chaser in a coroner's court blush with shame." In one of his speeches he said:

The first railroad robbery was committed on the Rock Island back in 1873 just east of Council Bluffs, Iowa. The man who committed that robbery used a gun and a horse and got up early in the morning. He and his gang took a chance of being killed and eventually most were. That railroad robber's name was Jesse James. The same Jesse James held up the Missouri Pacific in 1876 and took the paltry sum of seventeen thousand dollars from the express car. About thirty years after the Council Bluffs holdup, the Rock Island went through a looting by some gentlemen known as the "Tin Plate Millionaires." They used no guns but they ruined the railroad and got away with seventy million dollars or more. They did it by means of holding companies. Senators can see what "pikers" Mr. James and his crowd were alongside of some real artists.

Speech to the Senate
June 3, 1937

One of the difficulties, as I see it, is that we worship money instead of honor. . . . No one ever considered Carnegie libraries steeped in the blood of the Homestead steel workers, but they are. We do not remember that the Rockefeller Foundation is founded on the dead miners of the Colorado Fuel & Iron Company and a dozen other similar performances. We worship mammon; and until we go back to ancient fundamentals and return to the Giver of the Tables of the Law and His teachings, these conditions are going to remain with us.

Speech to Congress
December 20, 1937

During a labor dispute in the railroad industry, Truman's Administration had managed to negotiate settlements with eighteen of the twenty unions involved. The heads of the two remaining unions sent word to the President that their members would strike on May 18. Truman called them to the White House and said:

If you think I'm going to sit here and let you tie up this country, you're crazy as hell. I am going to protect the public and we are going to run these railroads and you can put that in your pipe and smoke it!

The White House
May, 1946

He [John L. Lewis] cannot face the music when the tune is not to his liking.

Memorandum of December 11, 1946
in Mr. President
by William Hillman

In September of 1950, in response to a Senator's suggestion that he name John L. Lewis Ambassador to the Soviet Union, Truman replied:

I wouldn't appoint Lewis to be dog catcher.

LIBERALISM
VERSUS CONSERVATISM

Now, rugged individualism means rugged individualism. It means the bold and ruthless individualism that would rise above law and morals, above human equities and decencies allowing no consideration of the rights of nonrugged individuals to stand in the way of success. Happily for us at this time, we have few rugged individualists left aside from Senator Patterson [his opponent]. . . .

Senate campaign speech
Missouri
September 11, 1934

The rugged individualists among the Republican speakers have talked a great deal about the cost of the New Deal. I have never heard one of them ever speak derogatorily of the cost of the World War. . . .

I do not understand a mind which sees a gracious benefice in spending money to slay and maim human beings in almost unimaginable amounts and deprecates the expenditure of a smaller sum to patch up the ills of erring mankind.

Senate campaign speech
Jackson County, Missouri
October 12, 1934

All of you, I am sure, have heard many cries about Government interference with business and about "creeping socialism." I should like to remind the gentlemen who make these complaints that if events had been allowed to continue as they were going prior to March 4, 1933, most of them would have no businesses left for the Government or anyone else to interfere with—and almost surely we would have socialism in this country, real socialism.

Detroit
May 14, 1950

We cannot drive scientists into our laboratories, but, if we tolerate reckless or unfair attacks, we can certainly drive them out.

About McCarthyism:

I charge that the Republicans have impeded and made more difficult our efforts to cope with Communism in the country.

I charge that they have hindered the efforts of the FBI, which has been doing wonderful work in protecting the national security.

I charge that the Republicans have attempted to usurp

the constitutional functions of federal grand juries and courts.

I charge that they have not produced any significant information about Communist espionage which the FBI did not already have.

I charge the Republicans with having impaired our nation's atomic energy program by their intemperate and unjustified attacks on our atomic scientists.

I charge them with having recklessly cast a cloud of suspicion over the most loyal civil service in the world.

I charge them with having trampled on the individual freedoms which distinguish American ideals from totalitarian doctrine.

I charge finally that, in all this, they have not hurt the Communist Party. They have helped it.

Oklahoma City, Oklahoma
September 29, 1948

McCarthyism . . . the meaning of the word is the corruption of truth, the abandonment of our historical devotion to fair play. It is the abandonment of "due process" of law. It is the use of the big lie and the unfounded accusation against any citizen in the name of Americanism and security. It is the rise to power of the demagogue who lives on untruth; it is the spread of fear and the destruction of faith in every level of our society.

My friends, this is not a partisan matter. This horrible cancer is eating at the vitals of America and it can destroy the great edifice of freedom.

Radio and television address
Kansas City, Missouri
November 17, 1953

In December of 1947, the newspapers rumored that Truman was sick. One night the healthy President wrote a memorandum to which he attached the news clippings.

I have just made some additions to my Kitchen Cabinet, which I will pass on to my successor in case the Cow should fall when she goes over the moon.

Among the appointments to this Kitchen Cabinet were a Secretary for Inflation, a Secretary for Columnists and a Secretary for Semantics. He went on:

Then I have appointed a Secretary of Reaction. I want him to abolish flying machines and tell me how to restore oxcarts, oar boats and sailing ships. What a load he can take off my mind if he will put the atom back together so it cannot be broken up. What a worry that will abolish for both me and Vishinski.

Mr. President
by William Hillman

I don't care what your politics are, I don't care what you believe politically, and I don't care what your religion is, as long as you live by it and act by it. But you must watch out for these people who make mountains out of something that doesn't exist—not even a molehill! . . . the best way to handle them is to ridicule them. You know, there's no stuffed shirt that can stand ridicule. When you stick a pin in that stuffed shirt and let the wind out, he's through!

Lecture series
Columbia University
April 29, 1959

I have said many a time that I think the Un-American Activities Committee in the House of Representatives was the most un-American thing in America.

Lecture series
Columbia University
April 29, 1959

I have collected since I have been in the White House a great many stories about the improvement of that structure and about the various Presidents and First Ladies who have been in it.

There's a story around the White House that Mrs. Millard Fillmore brought the first bathtub into the White House. There is also a story in connection with it, that the local medical association in Cincinnati, Ohio, passed a resolution calling Mrs. Fillmore an indecent person because she had put a bathtub in the White House.

This medical association in Cincinnati said that it was unsanitary, that it was unhealthy, that no person should take all his clothes off at one time.

Well, my friends, there has been some progress since that date, and I want to say to you, there are more bathtubs in the White House now than there are in the Benjamin Franklin Hotel.

Speech to the American Hospital Association
Philadelphia
September 16, 1952

I know how you feel when you want to punch some old backward-looking fellow in the nose because he can't see the necessity for what has to take place.

From his letters and memoranda of 1951
in Mr. President
by William Hillman

About medicare proposals:

My only interest in this matter is better health for our people. That is why I have constantly asked the "pullbacks" to come forward with plans of their own. But you know it is a common failing of the "pullbacks"—they don't want to move ahead at all, no matter how it is done. They just want to stand still, with things as they are, or even move backward.

> *Speech to the American Hospital Association*
> *Philadelphia*
> *September 16, 1952*

I don't believe in anti-anything. A man has to have a program; you have to be for something, otherwise you will never get anywhere.

> *Lecture series*
> *Columbia University*
> *April 28, 1959*

At the opening of the Grand Coulee Dam, Mr. Truman said:

The dam had to be fought for. It had to be built over furious opposition. You remember what its opponents said . . . "Up in the Grand Coulee country there is no one to sell power to except the coyotes and jackrabbits and there never will be." . . . Today, those who opposed Grand Coulee are trying to cover their tracks. . . . But they can't erase the record. They did not understand then, and they do not understand now . . . that the United States is a growing dynamic country. They saw no need to plan and work for a greater future. The way things were was good enough for them.

Grand Coulee, Washington
May 11, 1950

About the proposed requirement that all students receiving government assistance be required to take a loyalty oath:

I think a test oath for students is silly. Teachers who don't know enough to teach you about our great government have no business being teachers, and after you've learned all you can about it, if you become one who doesn't appreciate his government, you are welcome to go to Russia or somewhere else, and then you can satisfy yourself.

Lecture series
Columbia University
April 28, 1959

There is nothing new in the world except the history you do not know.

FOREIGN AFFAIRS

Peace is the goal of my life. I'd rather have lasting peace in the world than be President. I wish for peace, I work for peace and I pray for peace continually.

Philadelphia
October 6, 1948

No nation on this globe should be more internationally minded than America because it was built by all nations.

Chicago
March 17, 1945

Don't talk about rope in the house of somebody who has been hanged.

Indianapolis
October 15, 1948

I still hope that some sort of a world arrangement along the lines laid out by Henry IV [of France] and Woodrow Wilson may be worked out. Eventually it will have to be, or our civilization will end as all other great civilizations have, and we'll just start over from another dark age.

Speech at Liberty Memorial
Kansas City, Missouri
November 11, 1938

In a series of talks with Molotov on April 22 and 23, 1945, the new President spoke harshly about the Russians' violations of the Yalta Agreement. He demanded that they keep their word.

We don't want to operate on the basis of a one-way street.

Molotov flushed. "I have never been talked to like that in my life," he grumbled. Truman snapped back:

Carry out your agreements and you won't get talked to like that.

On July 3, 1945—shortly before the Potsdam Conference—he wrote his mother:

I am getting ready to see Stalin & Churchill, and it is a chore. I have to take my tuxedo, tails . . . preacher coat, high hat, low hat and hard hat.

In the cause of freedom, we have to battle for the rights of people with whom we do not agree; and whom, in many cases, we may not like. These people test the strength of the freedoms which protect all of us. If we do not defend their rights, we endanger our own.

About recognition of Spain:

Spain had already been recognized at the time I became President of the United States. I never had any use for Franco. That's all that needs to be said. I never gave him any house. He wouldn't let a Baptist be buried in daylight. That's the truth. He had to be buried at night in plowed ground.

Lecture series
Columbia University
April 28, 1959

I know that Japan is a terribly cruel nation in warfare but I can't bring myself to believe that, because they are cruel, we should ourselves act in the same manner. For myself, I certainly regret the necessity of wiping out whole populations because of the "pigheadedness" of the leaders of a nation and, for your information, I am not going to do it unless it becomes absolutely necessary. My object is to save as many American lives as possible but I also have a humane feeling for the women and children in Japan.

From his letters and memoranda of 1945
in Mr. President
by William Hillman

It was the spirit of liberty which gave us our armed strength and which made our men invincible in battle. . . . And so on V-J Day, we take renewed faith and pride in our own way of life. We have had our day of rejoicing over this victory. We have had our day of prayer and devotion. Now let us set aside V-J Day as one of renewed consecration to the principles which have made us the strongest nation on earth and which, in this war, we have striven so mightily to preserve.

V-J Day radio speech
Washington, D.C.
September 1, 1945

The guns were silenced. The war was over. I was thinking of President Roosevelt, who had not lived to see this day. . . . I reached for the telephone and called Mrs. Roosevelt. I told her that in this hour of triumph I wished that it had been President Roosevelt, and not I, who had given the message to our people.

Memoirs of Harry S Truman

Almost two months have passed since the atomic bomb was used against Japan. That bomb did not win the war, but it certainly shortened the war. We know that it saved the lives of thousands of American and Allied soldiers. . . . Never in history has society been confronted with a power so full of potential danger and at the same time so full of promise for the future of man and for the peace of the world. I think I express the faith of the American people when I say that we can use the knowledge we have won, not for the devastation of war, but for the future welfare of humanity.

Message to Congress
October 3, 1945

I believe that atomic energy should not be used to fatten the profits of big business. I believe that it should be used to benefit all the people.

The largest private corporation in the world is far too small to be entrusted with such power, least of all for its own profit.

Milwaukee
October 14, 1948

Think what can be done, once our capital, our skills, our science—most of all, atomic energy—can be released from the tasks of defense and turned wholly to peaceful purposes around the world.

There is no end to what can be done. I can't help but dream out loud a little here.

The Tigris and Euphrates Valley can be made to bloom as it did in the times of Babylon and Nineveh. Israel can be made the country of milk and honey as it was in the time of Joshua. There is a plateau in Ethiopia. . . . Enough food can be raised to feed a hundred million people. There are places in South America—places like Colombia and Venezuela and Brazil—just like that plateau in Ethiopia— places where food could be raised for millions of people.

These things can be done, and they are self-liquidating projects. If we can get peace and safety in the world under the United Nations, the developments will come so fast we will not recognize the world in which we now live.

Farewell address
Washington, D.C.
January 15, 1953

More than half the people of the world are living in conditions approaching misery. . . . For the first time in history humanity possesses the knowledge and the skill to relieve the suffering of these people.

During 1946 and 1947, Truman worked steadily to help the Jewish people found Israel, but he was attacked from all sides. He wrote in a letter to Dave Niles concerning his frustration:

I wish God Almighty would give the Children of Israel an Isaiah, the Christians a St. Paul, and the Sons of Ishmael a peep at the Golden Rule.

Later he wrote to Mrs. Eleanor Roosevelt, then Ambassador to the United Nations:

The action of some of our American Zionists will eventually prejudice everyone against what they are trying to get done. . . . I regret this situation very much because my sympathy has always been on their side.

After Truman brought about recognition of the new country, Rabbi Herzog, the Chief Rabbi of Israel, went to the White House to thank him. David Niles recalled: "Rabbi Herzog told Truman, 'God put you in your mother's womb so you would be the instrument to bring about the rebirth of Israel after two thousand years.' I thought he was overdoing things, but when I looked over at the President, tears were running down his cheeks."

That Man from Missouri
by Alfred Steinberg

When Kansas and Colorado have a quarrel over the water in the Arkansas River they don't call out the National Guard in each state and go to war over it. They bring a suit in the Supreme Court of the United States and abide by the decision. There isn't a reason in the world why we cannot do that internationally.

Kansas City, Missouri
April, 1945

The United Nations was born out of the agony of war—the most terrible war in history. Those who drew up the Charter really had less to do with the creation of the United Nations than the millions who fought and died in that war. We who work to carry out its great principles should always remember that this organization owes its existence to the blood and sacrifice of millions of men and women. It is built out of their hopes for peace and justice.

Speech at the United Nations
October 24, 1950

Edward R. Murrow asked him what his most difficult decision in the White House had been. Truman replied that it was the ordering of the intervention in Korea. He recalled that as he acted he had remembered Munich and the League of Nations.

Truman: When the Republic of Korea was about to be overcome by aggressions started by the Communists, backed by Russia and what later became Communist China, it seemed to me that the proper thing was to establish the

United Nations as a going concern and that's what I tried to do.

Murrow: Any regrets?

Truman: Not the slightest—not the slightest in the world.

Interview with Edward R. Murrow on the
CBS television program See It Now
February 2, 1958

When President Johnson went to pay tribute to the former President on the establishment of the Harry S Truman Center for the Advancement of Peace at Hebrew University in Jerusalem, Truman spoke about the years since he had begun to fight the cold war. The speech was read for him by a friend.

It all seems to have been in vain. Memories are short and appetites for power and glory are insatiable. Old tyrants depart. New ones take their place. Old allies become the foe. The recent enemy becomes the friend. It is all very baffling and trying, [but] we cannot lose hope, we cannot despair. For it is all too obvious that if we do not abolish war on this earth, then surely, one day, war will abolish us from the earth.

Independence, Missouri
January 25, 1966

HIMSELF

Early in 1953 in San Francisco, Truman was on his way to dinner at a friend's house. His chauffeur lost his way and the former President got out and rang a doorbell to ask directions. The man who opened the door didn't know where Truman's friend lived, but said, "By the way, I hope I'm not hurting your feelings but you look exactly like that old s.o.b. Harry Truman." Truman replied:

I hope I'm not hurting your feelings either. But I *am* that s.o.b.

I am just as happy as I can be, trying to be a private citizen and it's a hell of a job.

National Press Club
Washington, D.C.
May 10, 1954

I've always been sorry I did not get a university education in the regular way. But I got it in the Army the hard way—and it stuck.

In May, 1946, Margaret graduated from college. On that occasion her father made the commencement address and was awarded an honorary LL.D. degree.

It took Margaret four years, but it took me only four minutes.

Reporter: Is it as windy in Independence as it is in Washington?

Truman: It is when I'm there.

> *National Press Club*
> *Washington, D.C.*
> *May 10, 1954*

For a long time now, some of my North Carolina friends have been telling me I ought to take a look at this great State Fair of yours. It wasn't necessary to urge me very much. I have always liked to attend fairs.

But now I do have one complaint. Now they make me one of the exhibits, and I don't get a chance to look at the others very much. . . .

I don't mind being an exhibit here myself. I think I belong right here. I'm a home-grown American farm product.

> *North Carolina State Fair*
> *Raleigh*
> *October 19, 1948*

I wonder if it may not be such simple characters as Tom Sawyer and Huckleberry Finn who will, as symbols, show the world our undying contribution to the civilization on our continent. . . .

While intolerance is running rampant throughout the world, we need more friendly people, like those who grew so naturally out of the mind of Mark Twain, that kindly humorist from Hannibal, to guide us back to basic principles. . . . No matter how grave the postwar problems may be, I am sure that our American sense of proportion and—yes—our sense of humor, will see us through to victory.

Jefferson City, Missouri
February 22, 1945

He loved to quote Twain's remark, "If we had less statesmanship, we could get along with fewer battleships," and on his desk in the White House the only memento was a plaque with Mark Twain's words: "Always be good. This will gratify some people and astonish the rest."

Now Missouri has had a number of notorious characters. The three, I guess, most notorious are Mark Twain, Jesse James, and me. Mark and Jesse are dead and I have to fill in for them, so here I am.

Lecture series
Columbia University
April 27, 1959

As you know, I speak plainly sometimes—in fact, I speak bluntly sometimes and I am going to speak plainly and bluntly today.

September 7, 1948

One morning at his 8:00 A.M. *breakfast during his March, 1950, vacation on the Keys off Florida, the President began to recite poetry.*

> "The time has come," the Walrus said,
>   "To talk of many things:
> Of shoes—and ships—and sealing-wax—
>   Of cabbages—and kings—
> And why the sea is boiling hot—
>   And whether pigs have wings."

The presidential assistants listened throughout the recital of Lewis Carroll's poems—then one of them handed Mr. Truman the following poem by John Godfrey Saxe—"The Puzzled Census Taker":

> "Got any boys?" the marshal said to a lady from over the
>   Rhine.
> And the lady shook her flaxen head and civilly answered,
>   "Nein."

> "Husband of course?" the marshal said to the lady from
>   over the Rhine.
> And again the lady shook her head and civilly answered,
>   "Nein."

The President commented that this would surely be quoted often in the next days, since this was the first day of the 1950 census.

There are two schools of thought on the pronunciation of the state from which I come. Most of us who live along the Missouri River pronounce it with the "i" just as you

did. Some of our deep southern sections in southeast and south Missouri use the "a." In the old days the word with the "a" ending was sometimes used as the first name for a young lady.

From his letters and memoranda of 1947
in Mr. President
by William Hillman

I heard a fellow tell a story about how he felt when he had to make speeches. He said when he has to make a speech, he felt like the fellow who was at the funeral of his wife, and the undertaker had asked him if he would ride down to the cemetery in the same car with his mother-in-law. He said, "Well, I can do it, but it's just going to spoil the whole day for me."

Campaign speech
Dexter, Iowa
September 18, 1948

Once after the Harry S Truman Library was built in 1957 on the outskirts of Independence, Missouri, the former President took two visitors into the nonpublic lobby and played a classical piece on the piano there. The visitors were duly impressed, but as he finished he turned to them and said:

If I hadn't been President of the United States, I probably would have ended up as a piano player in a bawdy-house.

That Man from Missouri
by Alfred Steinberg

About "The Missouri Waltz":

It's a ragtime song and if you let me say what I think, I don't give a damn about it, but I can't say it out loud because it's the song of Missouri. It's as bad as "The Star Spangled Banner" as far as music is concerned.

Interview with Edward R. Murrow on the
CBS television program See It Now
February 2, 1958

His informal manner often shocked Washington after he became President. Once at a county fair he mingled with the crowd discussing local political problems with the farmers, whom he asked to call him "Harry." When an old American Legion locomotive came by, he ran into the street to toot its whistle. He played the piano for a group of Methodist ladies and winked at them as he said:

When I played this, Stalin signed the Potsdam Agreement.

Caruthersville, Missouri
October, 1945

He was always very critical of his own speeches. After one of them he said:

Well, the speech seems to have made a hit according to all the papers. Shows you never can tell. I thought it was rotten.

Once Harry Truman tried to raise a beard, but gave it up because:

The hair on the right side of my face grew upward and on the left side it grew down.

After Truman first became President, the reporters had a difficult time getting used to his early-morning walks. When he saw the reporters standing in front of Blair House at six one morning, he stopped and warned them:

Stick with me—I haven't started to get up early yet.

In Key West in March of 1950, he often entertained quite late into the evening, but he still rose early. He would walk around the island for a half hour or so chatting with Marines and sailors he encountered on the streets. One morning he also ventured into the bachelor officers' quarters, hoping to surprise people. He did.

Trying various doors like a military man making an inspection, Mr. Truman found only one man astir—and he was completely un-uniformed. In addition the man was all wet. He blushed and reached for a towel. The President had walked into the shower room.

After an operation:

They are all still trying to hold me down. The doctor still has his foot on my neck and he's getting a lot of help from Mrs. Truman and Margaret.

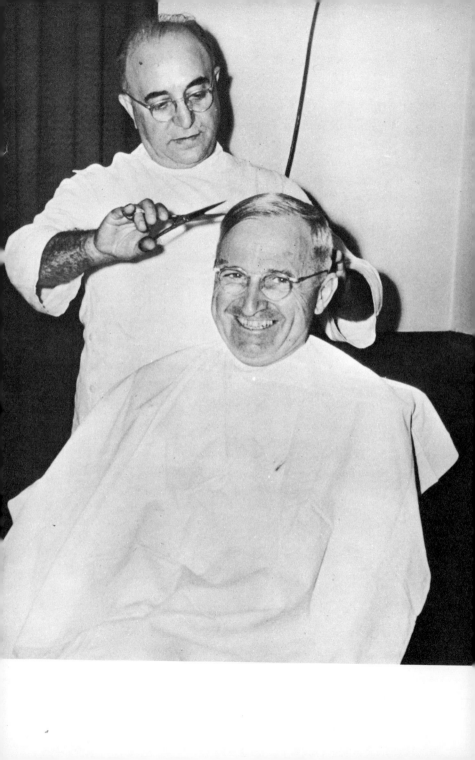

During the 1948 whistle-stop tour, a woman in one crowd commented about Truman's dimples. "Not dimples, they're wrinkles," Truman called back. "You can't have dimples at sixty-four."

"If you call those wrinkles," the woman replied, "then you are too old."

The President answered, "Now you're speaking for yourself, not me."

If I felt any better, I couldn't stand it.

Washington, D.C.
June 3, 1948

On board the ship Augusta, *the first afternoon at sea Truman told his staff he wanted to "go out on the front porch for a while." When he was kidded about his use of the term "front porch," he replied:*

The only time I was at sea before was going to France and back in the last war. Now, wouldn't it be silly for me to ape the language of men whose business is ships?

Thank You, Mr. President
by A. Merriman Smith

About hunting:

I do not believe in shooting at anything that cannot shoot back.

Mr. Citizen
by Truman, 1960

On October 12, 1944, during the vice-presidential cam-
paign, a New Orleans newsman, trying to make a story
about Truman's reputed poker playing, got this reply:

Card games? The only game I know anything about is
that game—let me see—I don't know what the name is,
but you put one card face down on the table and four
face up, and you bet.

My favorite animal is the mule. He has more sense than
a horse. He knows when to stop eating—and when to stop
working.

Mr. Citizen
by Truman, 1960

We can't be leaders of the free world and draw a color
line on opportunity.

Interview with Edward R. Murrow on the
CBS television program See It Now
February 2, 1958

A Democratic Representative from Louisiana, F. Edward
Hebert, made a suggestion that the Sunday preceding
Christmas be designated as a national day of prayer. Tru-
man replied in a letter of December 7, 1950:

I am extremely sorry that the sentiments expressed in
your letter were not thought of before November 7, when
the campaign in your state, Utah, North Carolina, Illinois
and Indiana was carried on in a manner that was as low as
I've ever seen and I've been in this game since 1906.

Mr. Truman also referred the Representative to his Thanksgiving Proclamation filed with the Secretary of State on October 20, 1950. He had said in part:

Again I ask all my countrymen to appeal to the most High, that the God of our fathers who has blessed this land beyond all others will in his infinite mercy grant to all nations that peace which the world cannot give. I entreat them in church, chapel and synagogue, in their homes and in the busy walks of life, every day and everywhere to pray for peace.

At one point in Truman's career, his political enemies spread the false rumor that since his grandfather was named Solomon, he was Jewish. Truman replied:

My Grandfather Young belonged to no church, but he supported many of them—Baptist, Methodist, Campbellite, and Presbyterian. They all met in the old church out in front of the house on the family farm on Sunday.

Truman went on to explain that when he was six he wanted to know which sect was best, and he quoted his grandfather as explaining:

"All of them want to arrive at the same place, but they have to fight to see who has the inside track with Almighty. When a man spends Saturday night and Sunday doing too much howling and praying you had better go home and lock your smokehouse."

During the 1944 vice-presidential campaign:

I am not Jewish, but if I were I would not be ashamed of it.

I rather think there is an immense shortage of Christian charity among so-called Christians.

From his letters and memoranda of 1950
in Mr. President
by William Hillman

His favorite prayer:

Oh! Almighty and Everlasting God, Creator of Heaven, Earth and the Universe:

Help me to be, to think, to act what is right, because it is right; make me truthful, honest and honorable in all things; make me intellectually honest for the sake of right and honor and without thought of reward to me. Give me the ability to be charitable, forgiving and patient with my fellow men—help me to understand their motives and their shortcomings—even as thou understandest mine! Amen, Amen, Amen.

A HAWTHORN BOOK